W9-AKC-169

Robert E. Lee

Confederate General

Colonial Leaders

Lord Baltimore
English Politician and Colonist

Benjamin Banneker
American Mathematician and Astronomer

Sir William Berkeley
Governor of Virginia

William Bradford
Governor of Plymouth Colony

Jonathan Edwards
Colonial Religious Leader

Benjamin Franklin
American Statesman, Scientist, and Writer

Anne Hutchinson
Religious Leader

Cotton Mather
Author, Clergyman, and Scholar

Increase Mather
Clergyman and Scholar

James Oglethorpe
Humanitarian and Soldier

William Penn
Founder of Democracy

Sir Walter Raleigh
English Explorer and Author

Caesar Rodney
American Patriot

John Smith
English Explorer and Colonist

Miles Standish
Plymouth Colony Leader

Peter Stuyvesant
Dutch Military Leader

George Whitefield
Clergyman and Scholar

Roger Williams
Founder of Rhode Island

John Winthrop
Politician and Statesman

John Peter Zenger
Free Press Advocate

Revolutionary War Leaders

John Adams
Second U.S. President

Ethan Allen
Revolutionary Hero

Benedict Arnold
Traitor to the Cause

King George III
English Monarch

Nathanael Greene
Military Leader

Nathan Hale
Revolutionary Hero

Alexander Hamilton
First U.S. Secretary of the Treasury

John Hancock
President of the Continental Congress

Patrick Henry
American Statesman and Speaker

John Jay
First Chief Justice of the Supreme Court

Thomas Jefferson
Author of the Declaration of Independence

John Paul Jones
Father of the U.S. Navy

Lafayette
French Freedom Fighter

James Madison
Father of the Constitution

Francis Marion
The Swamp Fox

James Monroe
American Statesman

Thomas Paine
Political Writer

Paul Revere
American Patriot

Betsy Ross
American Patriot

George Washington
First U.S. President

Famous Figures of the Civil War Era

Jefferson Davis
Confederate President

Frederick Douglass
Abolitionist and Author

Ulysses S. Grant
Military Leader and President

Stonewall Jackson
Confederate General

Robert E. Lee
Confederate General

Abraham Lincoln
Civil War President

William Sherman
Union General

Harriet Beecher Stowe
Author of Uncle Tom's Cabin

Sojourner Truth
Abolitionist, Suffragist, and Preacher

Harriet Tubman
Leader of the Underground Railroad

Robert
E. Lee

Confederate General

Patricia A. Grabowski

Arthur M. Schlesinger, jr.
Senior Consulting Editor

Chelsea House Publishers

Philadelphia

Produced by 21st Century Publishing and Communications, Inc.
New York, NY. http://www.21cpc.com

CHELSEA HOUSE PUBLISHERS
Production Manager Pamela Loos
Art Director Sara Davis
Director of Photography Judy L. Hasday
Managing Editor James D. Gallagher
Senior Production Editor J. Christopher Higgins

Staff for *ROBERT E. LEE*
Project Editor Anne Hill
Associate Art Director Takeshi Takahashi
Series Design Keith Trego

The Chelsea House World Wide Web address is
http://www.chelseahouse.com

First Printing
1 3 5 7 9 8 6 4 2

Library of Congress Cataloging-in-Publication Data

Grabowski, Patricia A.
    Robert E. Lee / Patricia A. Grabowski.
        p.   cm. — (Famous figures of the Civil War era)
    Includes bibliographical references (p.   ) and index.
    ISBN 0-7910-6000-4 (HC) — ISBN 0-7910-6138-8 (PB)
        1. Lee, Robert E. (Robert Edward), 1807-1870—Juvenile literature.
2. Generals—Confederate States of America—Biography—Juvenile literature. 3. Confederate States of America. Army—Biography—Juvenile
literature. 4. United States—History—Civil War, 1861-1865—Juvenile
literature. [1. Lee, Robert E. (Robert Edward), 1807-1870. 2. Generals.
3. United States—History—Civil War, 1861-1865.] I. Title. II. Series.

E467.1.L4 G55 2000
973.7'3'092—dc21
[B]   00-038388
                                                                  CIP

Publisher's Note: In Colonial, Revolutionary War, and Civil War Era
America, there were no standard rules for spelling, punctuation,
capitalization, or grammar. Some of the quotations that appear in
the Colonial Leaders, Revolutionary War Leaders, and Famous
Figures of the Civil War Era series come from original documents
and letters written during this time in history. Original quotations
reflect writing inconsistencies of the period.

Contents

1 A Fine Young Man   7

2 A Gentleman Soldier   17

3 A Difficult Decision   31

4 The War Goes On   47

5 Peace At Last   61

Glossary   72

Chronology   73

Civil War Time Line   75

Further Reading   77

Index   78

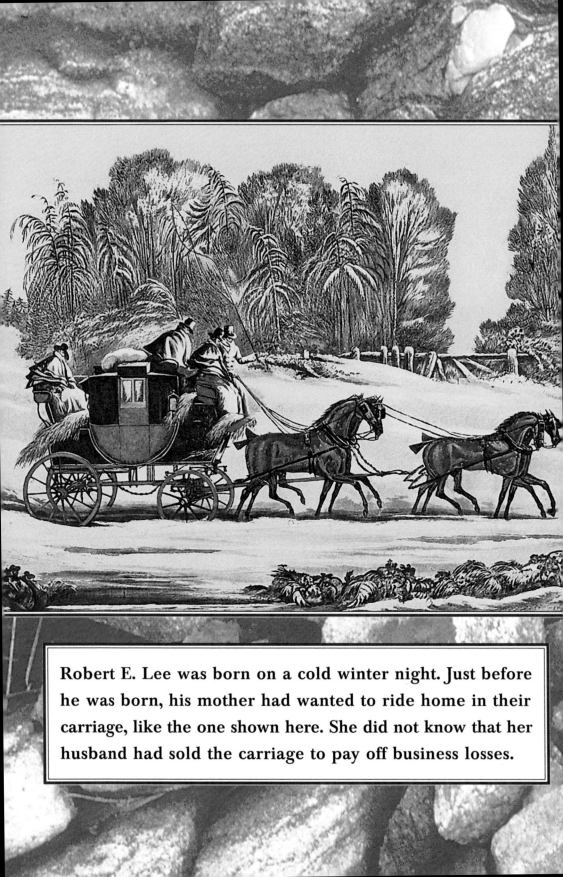

Robert E. Lee was born on a cold winter night. Just before he was born, his mother had wanted to ride home in their carriage, like the one shown here. She did not know that her husband had sold the carriage to pay off business losses.

A Fine Young Man

1t was almost winter when Ann Hill Carter Lee traveled to her parents' house, Shirley Plantation, on the James River in Virginia. It was a sad visit because her father had just died. She brought her three children with her: Charles Carter, nine years old; Ann, seven, and Sidney Smith, only five. Soon she would have another child.

The family stayed at Shirley for several months. As the time came near for Ann to give birth to the new baby, she decided she wanted to go home. She wrote to her husband, Henry, and asked him to send a carriage for her and the children. She didn't know that Henry had sold the carriage to pay some bills. Ann and her children had to ride home in an open wagon. It was very cold.

By the time they arrived, Ann had come down with a bad cold. Even though she was ill, she gave birth to a healthy baby boy on January 19, 1807. She named him Robert Edward after two of her brothers.

Ann Hill Carter and Henry Lee had married in 1793. They both came from very well-known Virginia families. Henry Lee was a famous Revolutionary War hero. He was nicknamed "Lighthorse Harry" because of his many daring deeds. He was a very good soldier. George Washington admired him for his courage and military skill. When Washington died, Congress asked Henry to write a speech about the first president. Henry wrote that Washington was "first in war, first in peace, and first in the hearts of his countrymen." These words are still remembered today.

Henry was governor of Virginia at the time he asked Ann to marry him. Ann was very happy

Henry "Light-horse Harry" Lee was a hero of the American Revolutionary War. Years later his son Robert also became a war hero.

because she loved Henry very much. But Ann soon discovered that Henry was not good at managing his money. He dreamed of becoming wealthy and made many business deals. He would buy land, not for his own use, but to sell it at a profit. Unfortunately, he usually ended up losing money instead. He was often in debt.

Ann was 17 years younger than Henry. She was his second wife. Henry's first wife, Matilda, had died in 1790. Henry and Matilda had had four children, but only two lived past childhood.

Henry and Ann went to live at Stratford Hall in Westmoreland County, Virginia. The house had belonged to Matilda. When Matilda died, she left it to her son. She knew how poorly her husband handled money. She wanted to be sure that Henry Jr. would not be left penniless. When Henry Jr. turned 18 years

Stratford Hall was one of the most beautiful houses in Virginia. It had 18 rooms, including a large ballroom. A grand staircase from the ball-room led outdoors to the garden below. Each room had a large fireplace. All the rooms were painted a different color. When the Lees moved out of Stratford Hall, the house was in very poor condition. Henry Lee sold most of the furniture to pay his debts. To save money, the family lived in only a few rooms. Many of the doors were chained to keep Henry's creditors from taking whatever hadn't been sold.

This is the house Robert was born in at Stratford Hall Plantation in Westmoreland County, Virginia.

old, he took charge of the house. Henry and Ann were forced to move.

Henry continued to have money troubles. When Robert was two years old, his father was arrested and sent to debtors' prison for not paying his bills. In 1810, after Henry was freed from jail, the Lee family moved to Alexandria, Virginia. Ann had many relatives there, and they were willing to help the Lees. Ann, Henry, and their children rented a house. Ann's father had left her a small amount of money, and she used it to support her family.

When Robert was five, Henry was badly injured in a fight. He had been defending a friend when a group of men attacked him. They poured hot wax into his eyes and tried to cut off his nose. He got better but was never really well again.

A year later, Henry left his family to go to Barbados. He said that he would return wealthy and in good health. Sadly, this was not to be. Henry wrote many letters to his wife and children telling them how much he loved them. But they never saw him again. In 1818, while he was on his way home, Henry became ill. He died in Georgia before he could reach Virginia.

While the Lees were living in Alexandria,

Robert attended school with his cousins. There were so many Carter children in Alexandria that they had their own school. The boys and girls were educated separately. Robert liked learning and did very well in school. When he was 13, he began taking classes at Alexandria Academy. He studied there for three years. Mathematics was his favorite subject.

Robert was very close to his mother as he was growing up. Unfortunately, Ann was not a healthy woman. She grew weak and could not get out of bed. She probably had a disease called tuberculosis. Robert tried to help. He was the only member of the family who could. His older brothers were away from home. His older sister was also in poor health. His younger brother was not old enough to do very much. The responsibility of running the house and caring for his sick mother fell on young Robert's shoulders. He did all the chores at home and kept up with his school work. As Ann's health worsened, he gave her medicine. He would lift her into her carriage when she had to go out. He had little time to do other things that he enjoyed. Robert would have liked to go hunting and play with his cousins, but he accepted his responsibilities and carried them out dutifully.

Even though Robert had barely known his father, he learned from his father's mistakes. He did not want to follow Henry Lee's example of letting down his family. Robert's mother loved her son very much. She gave him a strong sense of values. She taught him to be careful with money and to manage it well. She showed him how to love and care for his family and to treat them well. She also encouraged him to be proud of his country. He learned to stand up for his beliefs.

As Robert got older, Ann began to think about her son's future. She did not like the idea of Robert leaving home. "How can I live without Robert?" she asked. "He is both son and daughter to me." But if Robert was going to be successful in life, she knew she would have to let him go.

Ann could not afford to send Robert to college. The only way that he could get a free education would be to go to the United States Military Academy located at West Point, New York. The education there would be paid for by the government.

Robert would have no trouble meeting the requirements for admission. But before he could be accepted, he had to be appointed. For this, he needed a letter of recommendation. Only a small number of young men were admitted to West Point each year.

Ann and Robert asked their relatives for help. They helped him get a letter signed by some members of Congress. Andrew Jackson, who would be president one day, liked Robert and put in a good word for him. Robert was accepted at last. In June of 1825, after saying good-bye to his mother, Robert left Virginia for West Point.

At West Point, Robert and the other cadets learned to march in formation, like the soldiers pictured here. Robert worked hard and graduated second in his class.

2

A Gentleman
Soldier

Robert traveled to New York by train. There, he boarded a steamboat to West Point. He stood on the deck as the boat sailed up the Hudson River. The land on the west side of the river rose straight up and then became flat. The young man saw neat rows of tents on top of the cliffs. This was Camp Adams. Here he and his fellow cadets would spend the summer. The new cadets were called plebes. They lived outdoors, marched, and learned how to be soldiers. Each cadet was tested on school subjects. If he did not pass, he was sent home. Robert passed all the tests.

Life at the military academy was not easy. Robert was paid $16 a month in salary plus a very small allowance. This money had to pay for his uniform and other items. He needed to buy a mirror, wash basin, pitcher, pail, broom, and scrub brush. By the time he bought all these things, his money was gone.

In the fall, the cadets moved into the barracks. These were gray stone buildings with extremely small rooms. The cadets slept on mattresses on the floor. They washed with cold water in their wash basins. They ate the same things at almost every meal—boiled meat, boiled potatoes, bread, and butter. The food was often spoiled.

The students' day began at 5:30 A.M. They dressed quickly and reported for roll call. Breakfast was at 7. Classes started an hour later and lasted until 4 P.M. If the weather was good, the cadets practiced marching for two hours. After supper they studied more, then went to sleep at 10 P.M. The schedule was the same day after day. The cadets only had some free time on Sunday afternoons, Christmas, and New Year's Day.

There were lots of rules at West Point, and the cadets received **demerits** if they broke them. One rule was the most difficult for Robert. He was not allowed to leave West Point during his first two years. He would not be able to visit his mother. In addition, he was not allowed to drink, smoke, play cards, or read novels. Cadets were only allowed to read books that were needed for their studies. Robert followed all the rules. He did not get any demerits. His good looks and perfect behavior caused his classmates to nickname him the "Marble Model."

Robert was also a good student. He studied mathematics, drawing, French, and military science. He liked to read. He read more than he had to for his classes. In 1829, after four years at West Point, Robert graduated second in his class. He earned the rank of second lieutenant in the Corps of Engineers. He was also awarded the academy's highest honor—"**adjutant** of the corps of cadets."

Immediately following his graduation, Robert went home to take care of his mother, who was very ill. One month later, Ann Lee died. After his mother's death, Robert visited his cousin Mary Anne Randolph Custis. She was the great-granddaughter of Martha Washington. She and her parents lived in Arlington House, just outside of Washington, D.C.

In November, Robert reported to Cockspur Island, Georgia. This was his first job for the army after his graduation from West Point. He was in charge of building foundations for a fort on the Savannah River. It was very dirty and boring work, but he continued to visit Mary. In May 1830, Robert asked her to marry him and she agreed.

The following May, the army sent Robert to Fort Monroe, Virginia. One month later, Robert and Mary were married. They went to live at Fort Monroe, but Mary was not happy there. It

This painting shows people at a Southern wedding around the time of Robert's marriage to Mary Custis, the great-granddaughter of Martha Washington.

was very different from the large house where she had grown up.

When Mary became pregnant, she returned to Arlington to give birth to her baby. The couple had a total of seven children. Their first baby was born in 1832. They named him George Washington Custis Lee. Robert called him "Boo." Their second child was a girl named Mary Custis. She was called "Daughter." Soon after Mary Custis was born, Mary became very ill. She recovered, but was never quite the same. Their other children were born between 1837 and 1846. They were William Henry Fitzhugh, called "Rooney"; Anne, called "Annie"; Agnes, called "Wigs"; Robert E. Jr., called "Rob"; and Mildred, called "Precious Life."

Robert was not happy with his job. When the army offered him a new job in Washington, D.C., he immediately said yes. He worked in the Chief of Engineers Office. But, once again, he was bored with the assignment.

In 1835, the army sent him west to help decide the boundary line between Ohio and Michigan. A year later, he was promoted to first lieutenant. He then went to St. Louis, Missouri, to find a way to change the course of the

Mississippi River. His wife and the children joined him there. When Mary became pregnant again, she went back to Arlington. Robert succeeded in solving the problem with the Mississippi and was promoted to captain in 1838. Two years later, he was sent to Fort Hamilton in New York. His family joined him again but soon left when Mary learned she was pregnant once again.

In 1846, the United States declared war on Mexico. The United States and Mexico both wanted the same land. Robert thought that the United States was wrong to declare war. But for him, fighting in the war presented an opportunity to earn another promotion.

General Winfield Scott gave Robert the job of **scouting** the land to find the best routes to attack the enemy. Robert was very good at this. At Cerro Gordo, Mexico, he found a way to bring heavy guns up into the mountains. This was helpful as U.S. forces marched toward Mexico City. The city was well guarded. General Scott's

Soldiers prepare for a battle in the Mexican War. In Mexico, Robert's commanding general praised the young officer for his courage.

men had to strike quickly or they could be wiped out. The only way to attack was through an area called the *pedregal*. This land was covered with sharp pieces of broken volcanic rock, but

Robert found a way to cross. The U.S. troops surprised the Mexicans and captured the city. The war was over. General Scott was very pleased with Robert's work, calling him "the best soldier in Christendom."

Robert went home for a short time. From 1849 to 1852, he worked in Baltimore, Maryland. In 1852, he became superintendent of the U.S. Military Academy at West Point. While he was there, he made many changes and improvements. He took an interest in the work of each cadet. His family lived at West Point with him. In 1854, his son, Custis, graduated first in his class from the academy.

A year later, Robert was promoted to lieutenant

During the Mexican War, Robert and a fellow soldier were on a scouting mission. They stopped near a spring. Suddenly, they heard men speaking Spanish. Robert's friend ran away. Robert had only enough time to drop to the ground. He hid behind a big tree that had fallen over. Mexican soldiers kept coming to the spring all day to drink and fill their canteens. Some of them even sat on the log that Robert was hiding behind. He stayed perfectly still and quiet. When it got dark, he was finally able to escape.

colonel. He was named second-in-command of a **cavalry** unit at Camp Cooper in Texas. His job was to keep the settlers safe from Apache and Comanche Indian attacks. Again, he was not happy. Texas was very hot and dusty. He wrote to his daughter, "It is so hot in my tent now that . . . candles have melted, and become liquid in the stand."

In 1857, Robert received a letter informing him that Mary's father had died. He went home to Arlington to take care of Mr. Custis's **estate**. When he arrived, he found his wife unable to walk because of **arthritis**. Mary had to use a wheelchair. For two years, Robert stayed at Arlington to take care of his wife and the estate. He paid bills and supervised repairs to the estate.

According to his **will**, Mr. Custis wanted to free all his slaves within five years after his death. Robert did not believe in slavery, but he felt it was not fair to free the slaves without teaching them how to take care of themselves.

When Indians began attacking many of the pioneers' wagons (as shown here), Robert was sent to Texas to protect the settlers.

He put the slaves to work on the repairs. He did follow Mr. Custis's wishes. All the slaves were eventually freed.

By the late 1850s, Americans were becoming more and more divided over the matter of slavery. A preacher named John Brown decided to do something about it. He and his followers went to

This picture shows John Brown on his way to jail. As the commanding officer, Robert led the troops that captured John Brown.

Harpers Ferry, Virginia. They planned to steal guns and ammunition from the government. They were going to give the weapons to slaves throughout the South. They captured the **armory** and took some hostages. The state troops tried to get Brown to surrender. When he refused, the federal government sent for Lieutenant Colonel Robert E. Lee. Robert took command of the state troops and U.S. marines. He ordered them to charge the armory. After a short fight, John Brown and his men were arrested. Brown was put on trial for treason. He was found guilty and hanged. Robert returned to Camp Cooper in Texas.

Robert (left) confers with General Thomas "Stonewall" Jackson. Robert loved his country but decided to lead Virginia's Confederate army in the Civil War.

A Difficult Decision

In November 1860, Abraham Lincoln was elected president of the United States. Lincoln was a Northerner. Like most people from the North, the president was strongly against slavery. He did not want slavery to spread to new territories. Many Southerners felt the president did not have the right to tell the states what to do. In protest, South Carolina seceded from the Union in December. This meant that the state no longer wanted to be part of the United States.

Robert E. Lee was very upset by this. He did not think that slavery was right. He was also against secession. He wrote to his son, Rooney, "I prize the

Union very highly, and know of no personal sacrifice that I would not make to preserve it."

Robert soon made many sacrifices. After Texas seceded in February 1861, Robert went home to Arlington. In April he was called to Washington, D.C., to see an adviser to President Lincoln named Francis P. Blair and General Winfield Scott. They asked Robert to take command of the U.S. army. He did not want to be **disloyal** to the United States, but he did not want to fight his family and relatives, either. It was a very difficult decision.

On April 19, 1861, Robert found out that Virginia had voted to secede. The next day, he **resigned** from the U.S. army. General Scott told him, "You have made the greatest mistake of your life."

The states that seceded joined together to form the Confederate States of America. Jefferson Davis was chosen president. Richmond, Virginia, later became the capital city. John Letcher was the governor of Virginia. On April 22, Letcher asked Robert to take command of Virginia's army and navy. Robert agreed. He was given the rank of major general.

The next day, Robert rented an office to use as his headquarters. He began to organize the Confederate army. The men who volunteered to be soldiers were farmers and townspeople. They were not at all prepared for war. Some were just looking for adventure. Most did not own slaves. Many, though, wanted to fight to protect their homes and rights. They were expected to get their own uniforms and horses. Their weapons were very old. Cadets from the Virginia Military Institute trained them to be soldiers.

The Union army, on the other hand, was very strong. There were many more Union soldiers than Confederate soldiers. Northern soldiers were well trained and had enough food and supplies. The Union army had the newest weapons because most guns were manufactured in the North. The war between the North and the South would be difficult.

Robert knew all of this. He told his wife that "the war may last 10 years." Robert felt that the

South had little chance of winning. Even so, he was determined to do his best for Virginia. He sent troops to places in Virginia where the North might attack. Soldiers were posted at Norfolk, Alexandria, Harpers Ferry, and Yorktown. He asked Thomas J. Jackson to command the force at Harpers Ferry. Joseph E. Johnston commanded all the Confederate troops in Virginia.

On April 12 Confederate troops fired on Union forces at Fort Sumter in South Carolina. The Civil War had begun. In May 1861, Robert was promoted to general. He served mainly as an advisor to President Davis during the first year of the war.

Robert sent a large force to Bull Run Creek in Manassas, Virginia. Union and Confederate soldiers met there on July 21, 1861. The Battle of Bull Run was the first important battle of the Civil War. When the Confederate army defeated the Union troops, Southerners began to hope that they could win the war.

A week later, Davis sent Robert to western Virginia. Union soldiers had won several battles

Jefferson Davis (at the podium, center) speaks to the crowd of people at his inauguration as president of the Confederacy in Montgomery, Alabama.

there. However, a Confederate commander had been killed. Davis wanted Robert to regroup the men. But other Confederate soldiers were in the area, and their commanders did not accept Robert as their leader. Robert himself was not sure of his duties. He gave the other leaders some suggestions.

Together, they came up with a plan to attack the Union fort on Cheat Mountain. They would surround the mountain and attack the fort at the same time. The sound of gunfire from the first group would signal the rest of the troops to charge.

But then there was a misunderstanding. Albert Rust, the commander of the first group, did not attack, and the other Confederate troops retreated. Afterward, the fort was still controlled by Union soldiers. The Southern newspapers blamed Robert for this defeat. They said he was afraid to attack. They nicknamed him "Granny Lee."

In November 1861, Davis sent Robert to South Carolina to make the coastal defenses of South Carolina and Georgia stronger. Robert was upset by what he saw as he traveled south along the coastline. If the Union navy attacked, the Confederates would not be able to protect themselves. Under his supervision, the troops spent four months building forts and putting large guns into place. Robert hoped this would keep the Union navy away from the shore.

Several months later, in March 1862, Davis ordered Robert to return to Richmond and put him in charge of regrouping and reorganizing the Confederate army. Robert knew that many soldiers would soon be leaving the army because they had only agreed to serve for a short time. Many were tired of war and wanted to go home. He asked the Confederate Congress for help. He wanted the lawmakers to pass the Conscription Act, which required that all men between the ages of 18 and 45 join the army. The Conscription Act became law on April 16, 1862. Robert's sons, Custis and Rooney, were already in the Confederate army. His youngest son, Rob, also wanted to join. At first Robert refused the young man's request. A year later, he agreed. Robert took Rob to buy a uniform and supplies for him.

By April 1862, Richmond was in danger of being attacked. General George McClellan of the Union army marched 100,000 soldiers toward the city. People gathered their belongings and left their homes. On May 9, Davis met with his **cabinet**. Robert was invited to attend. Davis said they would have to leave Richmond. But Robert was determined to defend the city. He said, "Richmond must not be given up; it shall not be given up!"

Robert sent General Jackson and his troops to the Shenandoah Valley. There Jackson won several battles against the Union army and earned the nickname "Stonewall." General Johnston and his men fought the Union troops at Seven Pines. Johnston was wounded in this battle. Davis ordered Robert to take Johnston's place as commander. Robert gave his army a new name. He called it the Army of Northern Virginia.

By early June, Robert had a plan. He ordered his men to dig ditches around Richmond. He stationed 25,000 men there and then took 50,000 men across the Chickahominy River to attack McClellan from the right. He wanted Jackson's troops to march down from the north and attack the enemy from behind. Robert hoped this would wipe out the Union force. On the morning of June 26, he knew something was wrong. Jackson was not yet in position. Even so, Robert began a fierce attack. Fighting continued at Oak Grove, Mechanicsville, Gaines's Mill, Savage Station, White Oak Swamp, and Malvern Hill. It lasted seven days. The **campaign** became known as the Battle of the Seven Days.

Union troops were still threatening Richmond. Major General John Pope was in command of a large Union force near Washington. Robert split up his army. He sent Jackson north to confront Pope's troops and left a small force to defend Richmond. Then he and General James Longstreet

The battle at Malvern Hill was one of the worst defeats for the Confederates. Early on July 2, General D.H. Hill told Robert that the Union held a strong position on the hill. They had twice as many men and guns as the Confederates. Hill warned Robert not to attack. Robert and General Longstreet rode off to look for a better place to attack. A Confederate soldier caught up with them. He said the Union Army was retreating. Robert ordered his troops to charge the hill. Unfortunately, the information was wrong. The Confederate army was badly beaten. General Hill later said to Robert, "It was not war. It was murder."

followed Jackson a day later. They planned to surprise Pope by attacking from the south. Pope held his position against Jackson's men, who had come from the north. When Robert arrived on August 30, the Union army retreated. It was an important victory for the Confederate army. This battle became known as the Second Battle of Bull Run.

A few days later, Robert marched the Army of Northern Virginia across the Potomac River into Maryland. On September 9 he wrote his "Special Orders No. 191." He directed the army to split up and march off in four different directions. Unfortunately, a copy of his orders was found by a Union soldier. The soldier gave it to General McClellan. When Robert's troops arrived, McClellan was ready for them. Robert stopped his men at Sharpsburg, a town near Antietam Creek. The Battle of Antietam began early on September 17. By the end of the day, Robert had sent all of his soldiers into battle, but he was not able to stop the Union army. General A.P. Hill

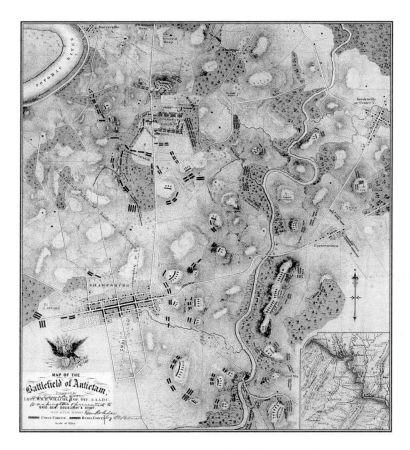

This military map of the Battle of Antietam shows Union forces in red and Confederate troops in blue. Robert's men lost the battle.

and his men arrived just in time to join the fight and save the Army of Northern Virginia. Robert marched his troops back to Virginia.

McClellan could have destroyed the Army of Northern Virginia by following them into

Virginia. But he let them get away. President Lincoln was not pleased. Soon after, Lincoln ordered McClellan back to Washington.

On September 22, 1862, President Abraham Lincoln announced his plan to free all the slaves in the South. His Emancipation Proclamation would take effect on January 1, 1863. This angered Southerners and made them even more determined to fight.

Ambrose Burnside, a Northern general, took over command of the Army of the Potomac. In December 1862, Burnside marched his army across the Rappahannock River near Fredericksburg, Virginia. Robert's troops watched

General Robert E. Lee was injured the day after the Second Battle of Bull Run. It was raining and he was wearing rubber pants and a poncho. He was standing next to his horse, Traveler. The horse's reins were wrapped around his arm. Suddenly, someone shouted, "Yankee cavalry!" The horse reared up on its hind legs. Robert tried to grab the reins and tripped. He fell and landed on his hands. Both of his hands were sprained. One had a broken bone. His hands were placed into splints. He had to keep one arm in a sling. Robert was unable to ride his horse for several weeks afterward.

from Marye's Heights above the river. They fired as the enemy crossed. Those who weren't killed fled back across the river. The Union army camped on the north side of the Rappahannock for the winter.

The Army of Northern Virginia spent the winter at Fredericksburg. It was a very hard winter. The soldiers needed clothes and shoes badly. There was not much food. And to make everything worse, Robert had recently learned that his daughter Annie had died of **typhoid** in October. He also had a bad cold, and for a time, had to stay in bed. He finally recovered early in April 1863. Soon after, he wrote to his wife, "I am feeble & worthless & can do but little." This was most likely the start of a continuing heart problem.

During the winter, General Burnside was replaced by General Joseph "Fighting Joe" Hooker. The Army of the Potomac had grown to 140,000 men. Robert had only 60,000. At the end of April, Hooker took his troops across the Rappahannock River. He planned to attack the Confederates and cut them off from their supply routes.

Robert knew he was outnumbered. He took a chance and split his army three ways. He sent General Jackson into an area called the Wilderness with 26,000 men. The Wilderness was a large forest with thick woods and vines. When the soldiers came out of the woods, Jackson would be in position to attack Hooker from the right side and from behind. Jubal Early was left with only 10,000 men to defend Fredericksburg against 60,000 Union soldiers.

Robert took the rest of the army and traveled west toward Chancellorsville. Hooker attacked on May 1. He expected Robert to retreat. He was surprised and confused when Robert did not. Hooker became frightened and ordered his army to fall back.

The Battle of Chancellorsville was a great victory for the South. Unfortunately, the Army of Northern Virginia also suffered a terrible loss

At the Battle of Chancellorsville (shown here), the Confederacy won an important victory but lost a great general, Stonewall Jackson.

during the battle. General Jackson was accidentally shot by one of his own men. The injury was very bad, and he died a week later. Robert was deeply saddened by the loss of his good friend and his best officer.

This portrait shows Robert in his Confederate uniform. He became the leader of the entire Southern army and he won many great victories for the South.

The War
Goes On

Large numbers of Union and Confederate soldiers continued to be killed in battles. However, Union troops were replaced more easily than Confederate troops because more people lived in the North. The Union also had the means to take better care of its soldiers. They got new uniforms and weapons when they needed them. Most important of all, the Union soldiers had plenty of food.

The South, in contrast, was running out of men. Robert's army was shrinking. Confederate soldiers could barely fight because they were weak from hunger. They needed clothing and shoes. Living conditions in the field were unhealthy. Almost as many men died from disease as they did by bullets.

On May 14, 1863, Robert went to Richmond. He met with President Davis and his cabinet. They talked about the war in other parts of the South. Union General Ulysses S. Grant, also a West Point graduate, was trying to capture Vicksburg, Mississippi. If he succeeded, Robert's army would not be able to get supplies from the western states. General Johnston needed soldiers to fight off Grant. Robert also needed more men. He wanted to win an important battle in the North. He thought it could help the South win the war. Robert knew his soldiers could get food and supplies in the North.

Once more, he crossed the Potomac River. This time, he headed for Pennsylvania. The soldiers marched through fields and farms. Robert told his men to pay for whatever they took. He warned them not to steal or destroy private property. He believed that civilians should not suffer because of the war. The soldiers paid with Confederate money. It was all they had.

Before leaving Virginia, Robert reorganized his army. He separated his troops into three groups, called corps. Each corps was also divided into three groups, called divisions. He sent a cavalry division commanded by J.E.B. Stuart to the Blue Ridge Mountains. Stuart was supposed to send messages about the position of the Union army. Robert hoped the Union troops would not see the rest of his army moving across the mountains. Unfortunately, Robert did not hear from Stuart and did not know the location of the Union army.

On June 10, Robert ordered the corps commanded by Richard S. Ewell to travel north. Longstreet left with his corps on June 16. Robert followed a day later with the third corps. He was still waiting to hear information from General Stuart about the Union army. But Stuart did not leave Virginia until June 28. When he finally got to Pennsylvania, he couldn't find the Union troops.

In the meantime, a scout named Henry T. Harrison met with Robert. Harrison told Robert that Union troops were coming from the south.

He also said that General Hooker had been replaced by General George Meade.

On June 30, a group of Confederate soldiers commanded by James Pettigrew marched into Gettysburg, Pennsylvania. They were looking for shoes. Confederate soldiers needed shoes very badly. When they got to Gettysburg, they saw Union soldiers, so they left quickly. The next day they went back. This time the Union army was waiting for them. On July 1, the two armies met at McPherson's Ridge. The Battle of Gettysburg had begun.

The troops fought for six hours before Robert even knew about it. He was still waiting to hear from Stuart. Robert rode into Gettysburg to see if he could get any news. He was surprised to hear gunfire. As he watched the battle, Ewell's troops arrived. They joined in the fighting. Robert and his officers watched from Seminary Ridge. Late in the afternoon, the Union army retreated up Cemetery Hill. Robert knew that taking control of the hill would be a great help in

The Battle of Gettysburg, Pennsylvania, (shown here) was the turning point of the Civil War. The South never recovered after losing so many men there.

winning the battle. He ordered General Ewell to take the hill. But in his message to Ewell, Robert used the words "if possible." Ewell thought Robert was giving him a choice. He chose not to attack Cemetery Hill.

That night, Union General Meade arrived

with the rest of the Army of the Potomac. This strengthened the Union position on the hill. Robert wanted to attack early the next morning. Longstreet was ordered to attack Union troops on Cemetery Hill and two small hills to the south. The two hills later became known as Big Round Top and Little Round Top. The sound of Longstreet's guns would signal Ewell to attack Culp's Hill. But Longstreet disagreed with this plan. He did not follow Robert's orders. He waited to attack until late in the day. Fighting took place in the Peach Orchard, Devil's Den, and Little Round Top. The Confederates were not able to drive off the Union army.

On July 3, Robert ordered Major General George E. Pickett to charge the center of the Union line on Cemetery Ridge. Pickett's division ran bravely toward the Union forces. In less than an hour, 10,000 men were lost and so was the battle. Robert blamed himself for this defeat. He spent that night planning the retreat. The Army of Northern Virginia headed back toward the Potomac on July 4. A 17-mile-long wagon train carried the wounded men. They crossed the Potomac River into Virginia on July 13. Robert wrote a resignation letter to Davis. Davis refused his request. The South needed him.

The South never recovered from the losses it suffered at Gettysburg. On October 15, General A.P. Hill, who had followed the Union troops, caught up with them, and launched an attack. The Union had many more men than Hill and won easily.

In late November, Robert prepared to fight General Meade near the Rapidan River. Meade decided that Robert's defenses were far too strong. He didn't think the Union could win the battle, and so he ordered a hasty retreat.

In December, Robert went to Richmond. President Davis wanted him to go to Dalton, Georgia, to command the Army of Tennessee. Robert convinced Davis that he was needed in Virginia. He recommended General Johnston for the job. On December 16, Johnston became

Ulysses S. Grant (shown here) took charge of the Union army in 1864. It took him almost a year to end the war.

commanding general of the Army of Tennessee.

While he was in Richmond, Robert visited his family. His wife was so crippled with arthritis that she could not leave her wheelchair. His son,

Rooney, had been taken prisoner by the Union. Rooney's wife was very ill and was not expected to live much longer. Robert also learned that Arlington House had been taken over by the federal government. He did not spend Christmas at home and soon returned to his headquarters.

Robert finally received some good news in February 1864. After eight months, his son Rooney was released from prison, exchanged for a Union prisoner.

In March 1864, General Grant traveled to Brandy Station to meet his new army. President Lincoln had just appointed Grant commanding general of all the Union armies. Grant was determined to stop Robert and to end the war.

The Union troops marched across the Rapidan River in the beginning of May. Robert waited. After the Union soldiers entered the Wilderness, Robert ordered Ewell and Hill to attack. This was in the same thickly wooded area where Jackson had defeated Hooker the year before. The Union soldiers became lost and confused in the thick

On June 8, 1864, General J.E.B. Stuart invited Robert to watch his cavalry parade. The men and horses were dressed in their best uniforms. Robert was happy to see his sons and nephews there. The next day, Stuart's troops was to begin a march across the Blue Ridge Mountains. Union troops stopped them. The Battle of Brandy Station was the largest cavalry battle ever fought in North America. During the battle, Robert's son Rooney was shot in the leg. Robert saw the wounded young man as he was being carried away from the battlefield and was glad to learn that his son would recover.

woods. They saw the bones of soldiers that had been killed in that first battle. Longstreet joined the attack the next day. The Confederates won the Second Battle of the Wilderness but not without paying a heavy price. General Hill had become ill and was unable to command his troops. General Longstreet was accidentally shot by his own men. He was not killed, but he could not lead his troops for several months. Robert was running out of experienced officers. He promoted Jubal Early commander of Hill's corps.

Grant's actions following the battle surprised Robert. Instead of retreating, Grant kept his army in place. Robert realized that Grant was planning to move his troops. With the help of some scouts, he figured out that the Union forces were headed for New Spotsylvania Court House. This was a small village to the southeast. Robert got there ahead of Grant. The Confederates drove the Union army back. Grant confused Robert by not continuing the attack the next day. Robert thought this meant Grant was going to move again. Robert made the mistake of moving some of his guns. The next day, May 12, Grant attacked. The battle went on for 16 hours. Robert found out that General J. E. B. Stuart had been shot that morning. He died the next night. Robert was very upset.

Grant headed southeast to Cold Harbor, Virginia. Robert's soldiers were ready and waiting for him. Grant was unable to get through the Confederate defenses. On June 3, 1864, the Union soldiers charged—6,000 of them fell in less than an hour. Grant would not accept defeat. Finally, on June 7, the two sides agreed to stop fighting.

At the Battle of Cold Harbor (shown here), over 6,000 Union soldiers fell in less than an hour. But neither side claimed victory.

Grant moved on across the James River. Again, Robert guessed Grant's plan. He was going to try to capture Richmond by going through Petersburg. Robert's men dug 30 miles of ditches around Petersburg. Some of the ditches were six feet deep. They dug caves and lived underground.

They also built forts connected by trenches. However, Union troops built forts and dug trenches as well. Both armies were prepared for a long wait. The **siege** went on for nine months. On January 31, 1865, Robert became general in charge of all Confederate armies.

That winter, Robert's army was starving. The soldiers were allowed only a small amount of food each day and suffered from **malnutrition** and disease. Their uniforms were torn and ragged, and they needed socks and shoes desperately. Many left because they could not take any more. Robert tried to stop them by ordering that deserters would be shot.

On April 2, Grant's troops broke through the Confederate defenses. There were no longer enough men to hold them off. Robert had no choice. He moved his troops out of the trenches. Union forces captured Petersburg and Richmond.

Robert (right) surrenders to Ulysses Grant at Appomattox Court House, Virginia. Robert's main concern was the welfare of his men.

Peace At Last

Robert knew that the end of the war was near. But he was not ready to give up. He ordered a retreat. He planned to join General Johnston and the rest of the Confederate army. As Robert marched his troops west, he hoped to get food for them along the way. The Confederate soldiers were weak from hunger. Their first stop was the town of Amelia Court House, Virginia. Robert expected to find food and supplies there. There were none. The soldiers had to get whatever they could from the nearby farms.

On April 5, Robert turned his men toward

Farmville. They were still searching for food. They marched all night. Once again, there was no food. They pushed on to the town of Appomattox Courthouse. There they met the Union troops and attacked. At first, the Confederates were able to drive the Union troops back. Soon, though, they were defeated.

On April 7, Robert received a letter from Union General Grant. In the letter, Grant strongly recommended that Robert surrender. But Robert wrote back, proclaiming he did not want to give up. Over the course of next two days, Grant and Robert wrote several more letters to each other.

When Union troops marched into Richmond on April 3, 1865, Mary Lee and her daughters were still living there. The city had been almost destroyed by Confederate soldiers. An ammunition building had exploded. Many houses had been set on fire. The Southerners didn't want to leave anything to the Union troops. President Lincoln visited Richmond the next day. He sent men to put out the fires near Mrs. Lee's house. Soldiers brought her food every day. A guard was placed at her front door to protect the family. She showed her appreciation by sending the young man a big breakfast each morning.

Robert spoke to his officers, some of whom still wanted to continue to fight. Finally, they all agreed that in the end they could not win the war. Very few Confederate soldiers remained. Most of the 28,000 men had not eaten anything in more than a week and did not have the strength to fight.

Early on the morning of April 9, Robert put on his best uniform. He tied on a red sash and picked up his sword. When he was ready, he said, "There is nothing left for me but to go and see General Grant."

Robert and Grant agreed to meet at the farmhouse belonging to Wilmer McLean. Robert was the first to arrive. He took a seat in the parlor. Grant kept him waiting for a half hour. First they discussed their experiences in the Mexican War. Then they spoke about the surrender. Grant told Robert that from then on the Confederate soldiers must agree not to fight the Union. Robert's men would be allowed to keep their horses and small guns. They would be allowed to return to their homes. The South would not be punished for the war. Robert was quite satisfied with the overall agreement. He thought it was very fair. Grant knew that Robert's troops were starving and offered to send them food. Robert accepted the offer and thanked Grant.

When the meeting was over, Robert stepped outside. He called for his horse and prepared to leave. Grant had followed him outside. He took off his hat as a kind of salute to Robert. Grant's soldiers did the same. Robert returned the salute and left.

Robert went back to his troops. He gathered them to say good-bye. He told them, "I have done the best I could for you." Robert's men loved and respected him. Most of them would have given their lives for him. Many of them did. He was a kind, caring commander who was sorry for all the lives that were lost. He thought of his troops as family.

On April 15, Robert rode into Richmond. He was finally home. Soon after he arrived, he heard

Confederate soldiers cry as they fold their flag for the last time. Robert was sad, too, because so many soldiers had died in the war.

that President Lincoln had been assassinated. A Confederate **sympathizer** named John Wilkes Booth had shot Lincoln in the head the day before, while Lincoln was enjoying a play.

General Johnston surrendered the Army of Tennessee to Union General William T. Sherman on April 18, 1865. By May 26, all Confederate troops had surrendered. The war was finally over, but the cost had been very high. In four years of fighting, nearly 650,000 Americans had lost their lives. Thousands more had injuries they would have to live with for the rest of their lives. The slaves that were now free had no homes, no jobs, and no education. Towns, farms, and businesses had been destroyed.

Robert spent the following few months resting. Robert hoped the South would begin to heal. He needed time to heal his own body and mind. He was sad and often sat quietly by himself. He also suffered many personal losses. His daughter, daughter-in-law, and two grandchildren were dead. His home and property at Arlington were gone. He had no money left. Robert desperately needed a job to support his remaining family. He wanted to set a good example for all Southerners by encouraging them to work hard to rebuild their homes and country. But he had to face a problem first.

On June 7, Robert was charged with treason. A grand jury decided he should be put on trial for fighting against the United States. Robert remembered the agreement he had signed at Appomattox. So he asked General Grant for help. Grant stood up for him and the charges were dismissed.

Although Robert was offered certain jobs at high salaries, he refused them. In August 1865 a group of people from Washington College came to see him. They asked him to become president of the college. Robert agreed, and he and his family promptly moved to Lexington, Virginia.

The college had only four teachers and 40 students when Robert took over, and the position paid only $1,500 a year. He worked very hard to improve the small school and soon more students started to attend. Under his leadership, Washington College became one of the finest schools in the country. After Robert died, the school's name was changed to Washington and Lee University.

In October 1865, Robert wrote to President Andrew Johnson. He asked for an official pardon. He wanted to become a citizen of the United States again. He had lost his U.S. citizenship when he joined the Confederacy. This meant he was not allowed to vote or run for office. President Johnson told him to write a letter stating his **allegiance**, or loyalty, to the United States. Robert wrote the letter at once. Unfortunately, the letter was lost after it reached Washington. It was finally found in the 1970s. Congress passed a law giving Robert back his citizenship in 1975–more than 100 years after his death.

In 1866 and 1867, Robert was called to Washington, D.C., several times. He was questioned about the war and the people who were in charge of the Confederacy. The government wanted to charge Jefferson Davis with treason. The charges were later dropped.

By the end of 1869, Robert was not well. His

heart problems had become worse. His doctor suggested that he take some time away from work. Robert and his daughter Mildred took a trip. They traveled by train through Virginia, North Carolina, and Georgia. Wherever he went, people cheered him. He was their hero. In Georgia, he visited his father's grave. He had been there only once before. He also went to see his daughter Annie's grave.

When he returned home, Robert asked the U.S. government to return Arlington to his family. But it had become a national cemetery. Many soldiers from the Civil War and other wars are buried at Arlington Cemetary.

The trip did not make Robert better. At the end of September 1870, he suffered a stroke. He spent the next two weeks in bed, only able to say a few words. His family stayed with him. On October 12, 1870, Robert E. Lee died.

During the last few years of his life, Robert had finally found peace. Working at the college was the most rewarding part of his life. Although he is

**This statue of Robert stands in Richmond, Virginia, as
a memorial to one of the South's most famous heroes.**

considered by many to be one of the greatest
military strategists who ever lived, Robert never
liked being a soldier. He often claimed that he

wanted to leave the army to live on a farm, saying, "I much enjoy the charms of civil life and find too late that I have wasted the best years of my existence." However, history will remember Robert E. Lee as both a great general and as a kind, gentle man who truly cared about people.

GLOSSARY

adjutant–a military officer who assists the commanding officer of a unit

allegiance–devotion or loyalty to a person, group, or cause

armory–a building where guns and ammunition are kept

arthritis–inflammation of the joints

cabinet–a group of advisers to the president

campaign–a series of battles in a war

cavalry–soldiers who ride horses

demerits–points accumulated for not following the rules

disloyal–not true to one's allegiance; unfaithful

estate–a person's property

malnutrition–illness caused by not eating enough healthy food

resigned–giving up an office or job

scout–a person sent out to look for the position of an enemy

siege–the action of surrounding a town to capture it

sympathizer–a person who shares the feelings or ideas of another

typhoid–a disease marked by high fever

will–directions written for the distribution of property after death

CHRONOLOGY

1807   Born Robert Edward Lee on January 19 in Stratford Hall, Westmoreland County, Virginia.

1825   Enters the United States Military Academy at West Point in New York.

1829   Graduates from West Point; mother dies; starts working for the U.S. army at Cockspur Island, Georgia.

1831   Marries Mary Anne Randolph Custis on June 30.

1840   Arrives at Fort Hamilton in Brooklyn, New York, to continue his work as an army engineer.

1846   Goes to Mexico to help General Winfield Scott during the Mexican War.

1852–56   Becomes superintendent of the United States Military Academy at West Point; promoted to lieutenant colonel; reports to Texas as second-in-command of the newly formed Second Cavalry.

1857   Returns to Arlington, Virginia, to settle the Custis estate.

1859   Leads federal and state troops to stop John Brown at Harpers Ferry.

1860   Returns to his command at Camp Cooper in Texas.

1861   Resigns from the U. S. army on April 20; agrees to command the army and navy of Virginia on April 22.

1862	Takes command of the Army of Northern Virginia on June 1; leads the Army of Northern Virginia in Battle of Seven Days, Battle of Second Battle of Bull Run, Battle of Antietam, and Battle of Fredericksburg.
1863	Leads the Army of Northern Virginia in the Battle of Chancellorsville, Battle of Virginia, and Battle of Gettysburg.
1865	Surrenders to General Ulysses S. Grant on April 9; becomes president of Washington College (now Washington and Lee University) on October 2.
1870	Dies on October 12 in Lexington, Virginia.

CIVIL WAR TIME LINE

1860   Abraham Lincoln is elected president of the United States on November 6. During the next few months, Southern states begin to break away from the Union.

1861   On April 12, the Confederates attack Fort Sumter, South Carolina, and the Civil War begins. Union forces are defeated in Virginia at the First Battle of Bull Run (First Manassas) on July 21 and withdraw to Washington, D.C.

1862   Robert E. Lee is placed in command of the main Confederate army in Virginia in June. Lee defeats the Army of the Potomac at the Second Battle of Bull Run (Second Manassas) in Virginia on August 29–30. On September 17, Union general George B. McClellan turns back Lee's first invasion of the North at Antietam Creek near Sharpsburg, Maryland. It is the bloodiest day of the war.

1863   On January 1, President Lincoln issues the Emancipation Proclamation, freeing slaves in Southern states. Between May 1–6, Lee wins an important victory at Chancellorsville, but key Southern commander Thomas J. "Stonewall" Jackson dies from wounds. In June, Union forces hold the city of Vicksburg, Mississippi, under siege. The people of Vicksburg surrender on July 4. Lee's second invasion of the North during July 1–3 is decisively turned back at Gettysburg, Pennsylvania.

1864   General Grant is made supreme Union commander on March 9. Following a series of costly battles, on June 19 Grant successfully encircles Lee's troops in Petersburg, Virginia. A siege of the town lasts nearly a year. Union general William Sherman captures Atlanta on September 2 and begins the "March to the Sea," a campaign of destruction across Georgia and South Carolina. On November 8, Abraham Lincoln wins reelection as president.

1865   On April 2, Petersburg, Virginia, falls to the Union. Lee attempts to reach Confederate forces in North Carolina but is gradually surrounded by Union troops. Lee surrenders to Grant on April 9 at Appomattox, Virginia, ending the war. Abraham Lincoln is assassinated by John Wilkes Booth on April 14.

FURTHER READING

Archer, Jules. *A House Divided: The Lives of Ulysses S. Grant and Robert E. Lee.* New York: Scholastic, 1995.

Cannon, Marian G. *Robert E. Lee: Defender of the South.* Danbury, Conn.: Franklin Watts, 1993.

Dubowski, Cathy East. *Robert E. Lee and the Rise of the South.* Parsippany, N.J.: Silver Burdett Press, 1991.

Kavanaugh, Jack, and Eugene C. Murdoch. *Robert E. Lee.* Philadelphia: Chelsea House Publishers, 1996.

Kerby, Mona. *Robert E. Lee: Southern Hero of the Civil War.* Springfield, N.J.: Enslow Publishers, 1997.

INDEX

Antietam, Battle of, 40-42
Appomattox Courthouse surrender, 62-64, 67
Arlington Cemetery, 69
Arlington House, 21, 23, 26, 55, 66, 69

Blair, Francis P., 32
Booth, John Wilkes, 65
Brown, John, 27-29
Bull Run, Battle of, 34
Bull Run, Second Battle of, 39-40
Burnside, Ambrose, 42-43

Chancellorsville, Battle of, 44-45
Civil War, 31-45, 47-59, 61-66
Confederate States of America, 32
Conscription Act, 37

Davis, Jefferson, 32, 34-35, 36, 37-38, 48, 53, 68

Early, Jubal, 44, 56
Emancipation Proclamation, 42
Ewell, Richard S., 49, 50, 51, 52, 55

Gettysburg, Battle of, 50-53
Grant, Ulysses S., 48, 55, 56-58, 62-64, 67

Harpers Ferry, 27-29
Harrison, Henry T., 49-50
Hill, A.P., 40-41, 53, 55, 56
Hooker, Joseph "Fighting Joe," 43-44, 50

Jackson, Andrew, 15
Jackson, Thomas J. "Stonewall," 34, 38, 39, 40, 44, 45
Johnson, Andrew, 68

Johnston, Joseph E., 34, 38, 48, 53-54, 61, 66

Lee, Ann (sister), 7
Lee, Ann Hill Carter (mother), 7-11, 12, 13-15, 19, 20
Lee, Charles Carter (brother), 7
Lee, Henry (father), 7-12, 14
Lee, Mary Anne Randolph Custis (wife), 20-22, 23, 26, 54
Lee, Robert E.
    birth of, 7-8
    and charge with treason, 67
    childhood of, 7-8, 11-14
    children of, 21-22, 25, 37, 43, 54-55, 66, 69
    and Civil War, 31-45, 47-59, 61-66
    and Custis estate, 26-27
    death of, 69
    education of, 12-13, 15, 17-20
    family of, 7-15
    and Harpers Ferry, 27-29
    marriage of. *See* Lee, Mary Anne Randolph Custis
    and Mexican War, 23-25, 63
    and official pardon, 68
    as president of Washington College, 67-68
    as superintendent of U.S. Military Academy, 25
    and surrender to Grant, 62-64
    in U.S. army, 20-26, 27-29, 32
Lee, Sidney Smith (brother), 7
Letcher, John, 32
Lincoln, Abraham, 31, 32, 42, 55, 65
Longstreet, James, 39-40, 49, 52, 56

McClellan, George, 37, 38, 40-42
Meade, George, 50, 51-52, 53

Mexican War, 23-25, 63

Native Americans, 26

Pettigrew, James, 50
Pickett, George E., 52
Pope, John, 39, 40

Richmond, 32, 37-38, 48, 53, 59, 64
Rust, Albert, 36

Scott, Winfield, 23-24, 25, 32
Seven Days, Battle of the, 39

Sherman, William T., 66
Slavery, 26-29, 31, 42, 66
Stuart, J.E.B., 49, 50, 57
Sumter, Fort, battle at, 34

United States Military Academy
(West Point), 15, 17-20, 25

Washington, George, 8
Washington, Martha, 20
Washington College, 67-68
Wilderness, Second Battle of the,
55-56

PICTURE CREDITS

page

ABOUT THE AUTHOR

PATRICIA A. GRABOWSKI is an elementary school teacher and freelance writer. She has degrees in music and education. This is her fifth book. She lives in Staten Island, New York, with her husband and daughter.

Senior Consulting Editor **ARTHUR M. SCHLESINGER, JR.** is the leading American historian of our time. He won the Pulitzer Prize for his book *The Age of Jackson* (1945), and again for *A Thousand Days* (1965). This chronicle of the Kennedy Administration also won a National Book Award. He has written many other books, including a multi-volume series, *The Age of Roosevelt.* Professor Schlesinger is the Albert Schweitzer Professor of the Humanities at the City University of New York, and has been involved in several other Chelsea House projects, including the COLONIAL LEADERS series of biographies on the most prominent figures of early American history.